the *7* lively sins

the 7 lively sins

how to enjoy your life, dammit

karen salmansohn

CELESTIAL ARTS
Berkeley / Toronto

A Kirsty Melville Book

Celestial Arts
PO Box 7123
Berkeley, California 94707
www.tenspeed.com

Distributed in Australia by Simon and Schuster Australia, in Canada by Ten Speed Press Canada,
in New Zealand by Southern Publishers Group, in South Africa by Real Books, in Southeast Asia
by Berkeley Books, and in the United Kingdom and Europe by Airlift Book Company.

Concept and book packaging by Glee Industries, formerly known as Amazon Girl, Inc.
Cover and book design by zinzell — www.zinzell.com

Library of Congress Cataloging-in-Publication Data
Salmansohn, Karen.
The 7 lively sins : how to enjoy your life, dammit / Karen Salmansohn.
p. cm.
ISBN 1-58761-173-2 (pbk.)
1. Women — Conduct of life. 2. Self-actualization (Psychology) 3. Seven deadly sins —
Miscellanea. I. Title: Seven lively sins. II. Title.
BJ1610 .S34   2003
179'.8-dc21   2002015145

First printing, 2003
Printed in Singapore

1 2 3 4 5 6 7 8 9 10 – 07 06 05 04 03

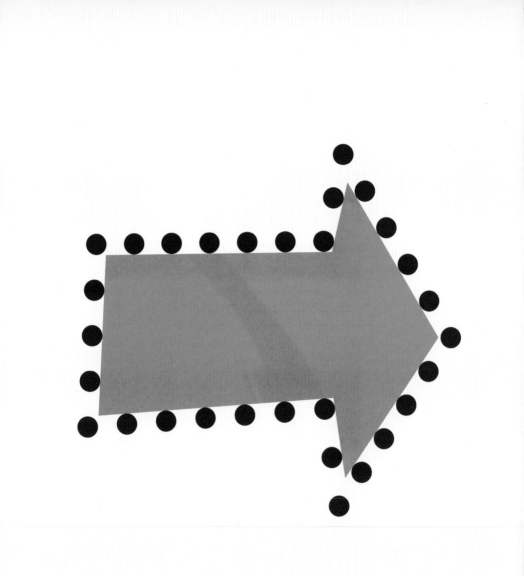

Silly YOU.

You used to be known amongst your friends as
"THE GREAT ENTERPAINER."

You loved to "enterpain" everyone with your amusing stories of disappointment, pain, woes, conflict, and miffed-ness.

And everyone laughed...ha,ha,ha... and begged you to tell them all yet another funny/sad/bitter/sweet plot development in that movie-for-one called your life.

During this time you even felt CONVINCED that your life NEEDED disappointment, pain, woes, conflict, and miffed-ness...IN ORDER TO BE INTERESTING.

And of course you wanted your life to be interesting.

Who wouldn't?

THE ANSWER:
5,678,389,261*
people in China, that's who.

*(Um, give or take 456,987,001. You forget exactly how many people live in China right now.)

In China, you've been told, they use the word "interesting" as a curse.

"May you live in interesting times," the Chinese tell a person they wish to punish.

Which confused you.

You wanted your life to be interesting...

NOT A PUNISHMENT.

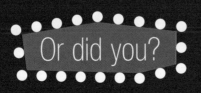
Or did you?

It was then that you wondered:

Did you —
on some secret level —
want to punish
yourself?

Did you —

on some secret level —
or even not so secret level —
feel guilty about
attaining too much —
too much pleasure,
too much enjoyment,
too much glee?

You thought
about this deeply…
and that's when
you realized
(CLUNK!)…

geez, you were a

SILLY YOU.

It's silly to feel bad
when you start to feel good.

And that's when you realized…

LIFE LESSON #1

You've got to stop with the enterpainment already! You deserve pleasure, happiness, glee, victory, joy, ardor, devotion, commitment, harmony, balance, comfort!

And all these can be interesting and entertaining — without all the enterpainment options. Lots of people enjoy stories with happy endings — and, dammit, it's time you became one of these lots. It's good to feel good about feeling good. Even when it comes to your love life. Especially when it comes to your love life.

That's when you also realized…

LIFE LESSON #2

LOVE MINUS PAIN

DOES NOT = PLAIN OL' LIKE.

LOVE CAN INDEED COME IN A PAIN-FREE FORMULA.

Sadly, you didn't always know this.

You used to joke, "I relate to those feisty Europeans who use the words 'passion' and 'suffering' interchangeably."

You used to joke, "If there IS such a thing as life on other planets, then the way we'll be able to tell if they're more advanced than us is NOT by asking to see their technology…but by finding out if they have dating. If they don't — then they're a more evolved species."

Yes, you were quite a kidder —

only you were never quite sure if you were kidding.

Yes, at this lowly point in your life
you no longer believed in attraction…
in fact you thought it should be renamed subtraction
because it had soooo many minuses.

Yes, you doubted lust could last.
Not only did you believe lust died…
you thought it deadly…a deadly sin.

Yes, you were a silly you.
Thankfully you aren't so silly anymore.

Now you know…

LIFE LESSON #3

JUST BECAUSE SOMEONE IS A CAUSE FOR LUST DOES NOT MAKE THEM A LOST CAUSE. LUSTING CAN BRING LOTS OF EVERLASTING, EVERLUSTING LOVE.

You can be lovable without being leavable.
Lust is not a foe…

Nor a faux friend.

Which brings you to…

LIFE LESSON #4

LUSTING DOES NOT DESERVE ITS LISTING AS 1/7TH OF THE WORLD'S MOST DEADLY SINS.

Lust is even quite lively…

helps your spirit feel quite alive…

When you act on lust you are acting on SPIRITUAL PRINCIPLES…because lust is an expression of WANTING TO CONNECT…TO EXPRESS STRONG LOVE…which is what the spirit is all about.

Lust is all about being FEARLESS, CURIOUS, AWARE, PRESENT…

Which brings you to…

LIFE LESSON #5

LUST (ding, ding, ding) SCORES BIG TIME BONUS POINTS BY REVITALIZING YOU WITH THE #1 SPIRIT ENLIVENER: MINDFULNESS.

You fully know and understand what lust is.*
But alas, you aren't so sure what mindfulness is.**

***Or rather over here:

Mindfulness: A spirit enlivening practice in which you empty your ego mind of its static…so you can better hear what your authentic spirit self is telling you beneath the ego mental ruckus.

*NOTE: Insert mischievous snicker here.
NOTE #2: So you decide to insert brief description here…*

29

Mindfulness — though seemingly not sexy — shares principles in common with lustful sex. You understand this further when you consider a little sexual metaphor…a little metaforeplay, so to speak.

A LITTLE METAFOREPLAY, SO TO SPEAK, IN A BOX

Sex is just a sweaty form of meditation. Think about it. The best lustful sex is about being in the moment, not obsessing about the past or future…or if your thighs look fat in a particular position…and so this means that orgasm is not the ONE AND ONLY big lure of lustful sex. A less obvious secondary benefit is that feeling of supreme peace that comes after sex — and this peacefulness isn't entirely due to reaching orgasm, but ALSO due to reaching one's metaphysical spirit, by being fully in the metaphysical moment. So when we feel good after lustful sex, it's partially because we've emptied our cluttered brain of its chattering.

WARNING!

Yes, lust is liberating on SO many levels, SO much SO… it comes with a WARNING…

Which brings us to…

LIFE LESSON #6

LUST HAS A NON-USAGE WARNING: If you DON'T express or act upon feelings of strong lust you can make your spirit weak…even kill your spirit… so you must let yourself get

lost in lust.

Which brings you to…

LIFE LESSON #7

Hmmm…if LUST is enlivening and not deadly…perhaps you should rethink THE REST OF THE DEADLY SIN GANG:

GREED

ANGER

PRIDE

SLOTH

ENVY

GLUTTONY

So you rethink about it and have a
VICE REVERSA REACTION.

You realize — for the same reasons that lust is a SPIRIT ENLIVENER — so are the rest of those reputedly deadly other guys.

Which brings you to…

LIFE LESSON #8

What's so deadly about GREED?

GREED IS ABOUT A HOPEFULNESS FOR GRABBING MORE OUT OF LIFE… AN ABUNDANCE MENTALITY… AN OPULENCE NOT ONLY OF MIND, BUT HEART AND SPIRIT…A DRIVE FOR CREATING…A WAY TO EXPRESS SELF-LOVE AND GIVE TO OTHERS. All of which is no deadly sin, now is it?

Yes, greed is A MAJOR SPIRIT ENLIVENER, helping you to BELIEVE AND PURSUE an endless flow of what you hanker for.

Sure in the end GREED can ALSO bring WADS OF CASH — but, hey, is it soooo bad to surround yourself with beautiful things?

Doesn't this show self-love — which your spirit supports?
Plus, Wads of Cash support loved ones — another pro-spirit endeavor.

Which brings you to…

37

LIFE LESSON #9

You believe in something called **abundance mentality,** an expansive outlook that puts forth that there's plenty to go around… so we should all be open to sharing the wealth — and serving as inspiration for others to garner wealth.

WE SHOULD ALL BE THINKING
LARGELY AND LIBERALLY.
All of this reminds you of a
KIND OF CORNY STORY...

A KIND OF CORNY STORY IN A BOX

Did you hear about the farmer with great ears? Each year his yummy yellow corn won blue ribbons in corn competitions. When asked his secret by a journalist, this farmer replied, "I share my corn seed with all my neighbors." The journalist baffled, asked, "Huh?!?!" The farmer smiled, and explained: "It's like this...the wind picks up pollen from ripening corn and cross-pollinates it from field to field. If my neighbors grow inferior corn, they lower the quality of my corn. Meaning, if I want to greedily grow the best-est corn ever, I must help my neighbors grow their best-est corn too."

You know the kernel of wisdom in this story:

We're all connected. What's good for you, is good for everyone. If you live with abundance mentality then you will indirectly (as well as oft times directly) help others to live with abundance too.

All of this gets you thinking…

LIFE LESSON #10

What's so deadly about ANGER*? ANGER IS ALL ABOUT A FERAL ENERGY THAT IMPELS CHANGE…NOT ONLY IN ONE'S PERSONAL SPHERE…BUT IN THE WORLD AT LARGE…IT IS A STIMULATOR FOR PRODUCTIVITY…AN ENERGIZING SPIRIT BOOSTER THAT HELPS YOU ACTUATE YOUR DEEPEST LIFE PURPOSE. No deadly sin in any of that, eh?

*dammit

Yes, anger is a force that awakens your spirit to action… creates a ferocious energy that can be channeled into demigod abilities to follow your spirit's truth and create a path to higher self-evolution.

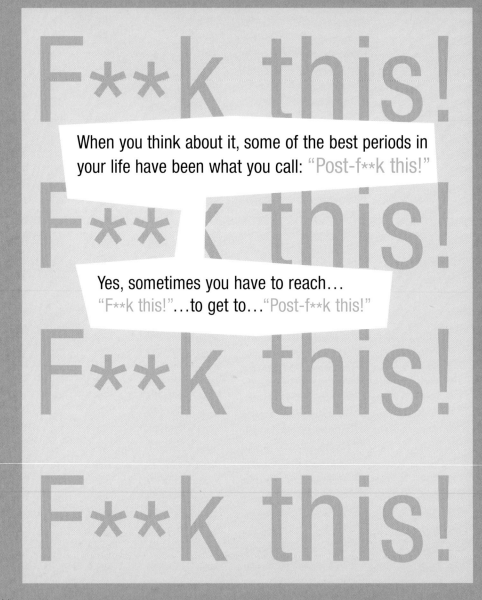

F**k this!

F**k this!

When you think about it, some of the best periods in your life have been what you call: "Post-f**k this!"

Yes, sometimes you have to reach…
"F**k this!"…to get to…"Post-f**k this!"

F**k this!

F**k this!

Post-f**k this!

Post-f**k this!

Post-f**k this!

P   s!

This is always a time of positive change
and growth…when you finally realize,
you're mad as hell…and you're
not gonna take it anymore,
cause you now (CLUNK!) see…

P   s!

Post-f**k this!

LIFE LESSON #11

It's better to be PISSED OFF
THAN PISSED ON.

It's better to SPEAK UP THAN BE TRAMPLED DOWN. It's better to FIGHT THE GOOD FIGHT THAN BE A GOODIE-GOODIE NON-FIGHTER WHO'S BENDING OVER BACKWARD AND NOT MOVING FORWARD.

Sadly you believe women in particular have trouble wisely wielding anger — and when women do, hell…hell hath no fury like a woman scorned — especially a scorned woman in spiky stillettos who now is motivated to kick a few cracks into that glass ceiling.

All of this reminds you of a story…

A DEAF STORY ABOUT A BLIND DATE

Your buddy David wanted to fix you up with his buddy Steve. After he got done describing Steve you asked David how he described you.

"I told him you were a victim," David said.
"What did you say?" you asked.
"I said you were a vixen," David repeated. "Is that bad?"
"No, no, not at all," said you.

IN OTHER WORDS:

Vixen = good

Victim = bad

IN OTHER WORDS:

Anger properly channeled and released can be a powerful force for a more fulfilling life.

Which brings you to an important pro-anger anti-corollary…

LIFE LESSON #12

Unreleased anger can be very deadly. You end up fuming… giving off noxious anger smoke that can be smelled a mile away…and so people stay clear of you. Plus, you end up getting your spirit all hot under the collar.

Yes, burning anger can be unsafe for both you and those around you if not wisely released.

Plus…here are…

TWO MORE BURNING ANGER WARNINGS:

1. BURNING ANGER NOT RELEASED uses up a lot of energy that could serve you better elsewhere.

2. BURNING ANGER NOT RELEASED garners you less, not more, respect, because you wind up being viewed as someone who doesn't (tsk, tsk) stand up for your rights.

Plus...

LIFE LESSON #13

Anger is not only a major spirit enlivener on a one-on-one, itty-bitty, individual-destiny level but in the grand-scheme of grand-groups…

Yup, anger has encouraged whole major civilizations and entire minority groups to actuate all the pro-active, pro-liberation changes they've been protesting for.

All of which gets you thinking…

LIFE LESSON #14

What's so deadly about PRIDE?
PRIDE IS ALL ABOUT SELF-LOVE…
SELF-RESPECT…
A DESERVED SELF-REWARD
FOR A JOB WELL DONE!
None of which is so deadly,
now is it?

Heck, if you don't allow yourself to feel pride, you miss out on appreciating life…fully witnessing the rewards of your inspiring, perspiring, aspiring efforts.

All of this reminds you of something Colette, the famous writer, once said: "What a wonderful life I've had. I only wish I'd realized it sooner."

Plus, it reminds you of something Karen, a not-yet-quite-famous-writer, once said, "Acknowledge is power."*

*(Um…er…okay, I take pride in saying I am THEEEEE Karen who wrote that particular phrase.)

Which brings you to…

61

LIFE LESSON #15

You need to give yourself an ACKNOWLEDGE EDUCATION, teach yourself how to acknowledge all the good you've brought into your life… focus on all you've got, and flaunt it, baby.

When you think about this, you think about something the highly quotable Baltasar Gracian once said: "When you have both talent and talent for displaying your gift, the result is something prodigious." You believe what Baltasar was promoting applies to promoting you. You must be your own PR agent…because…

CREATING COMMOTION = CREATING PROMOTION!

When you think about this you also realize…

LIFE LESSON #16

What's so deadly about SLOTH?

SLOTH IS ALL ABOUT THE PATH TO REJUVENATION…
SELF-RESPONSIVENESS…SELF-COMPASSION…
THE PURSUIT OF PEACE AND RELAXATION.
No deadly sin in any of that!

When you think about sloth, you think about that coyote and roadrunner cartoon. You feel sorry for that damn coyote. If only that coyote had recognized the virtue of sloth, taken a short, refreshing nap…he might have perked up and figured out how to catch that roadrunner.

You too have in the past felt like that foolish coyote… all caught up in today's fast motion/high commotion world…and this has prevented you from heading in the right direction because you are heading in too many directions.

When you welcome sloth into your life, welcome
SLOWING DOWN, LETTING LOOSE, RELAXING…
you find you gain clarity and make better life choices…

Get a better life.

Milton and Churchill — two big-time go-getters — are also two big-time stop-getters — two big-time spokespeople for sloth.

Milton wrote *Paradise Lost* while in bed. Ditto with Winston — who wrote those big bulky histories while supine, brandishing a bottle of brandy, to ease his writer's cramps.

Yes, it's ironic, but sometimes you have to slow down to speed up…stop completely to go **speedily steamrolling ahead.**

Meaning…

69

LIFE LESSON #17

You must learn not only to be pro-active…but pro-inactive. You must recognize when it's beneficial to be still, lie in bed, and do nothing… and really do nothing. You don't have to lie in bed and write a book like *Paradise Lost.* You can just lie there and GET LOST IN PARADISE.

You know…workaholism can be as toxic to your spirit as alcoholism.

IF YOU'RE WORKING HARD TO ACHIEVE SUCCESS, BUT DON'T HAVE TIME TO RELAX AND ENJOY YOUR SUCCESS, THEN, WELL, YOU ARE NO SUCCESS.

Meaning…

LIFE LESSON #18

Exhaustion is NOT to be confused for calm.

Only purposeful calm counts as calm.

With this in mind…you must stop your busy mind and schedule…take a deep breath and give yourself a 10-minute to 30-minute breather at various intervals throughout your day…or else…well… it doesn't take much of a sloth sleuth to deduce that…

lack of sloth = lack of energy
complete slothlessness = complete deadliness

Yes, yes, yes…sloth can be very enlivening to the spirit.

When you think about this you realize…

LIFE LESSON #19

What's so deadly about ENVY? ENVY IS A TRUTH BAROMETER FOR RECOGNIZING ONE'S DEEPEST DESIRES... A ZEAL THAT CREATES A DRIVE FOR IMPROVEMENT. No deadly sin in any of that, right?

Envy awakens your spirit to perk up to the lies your ego and upbringing have been whispering in your spirit-deaf ears about what you really want.

Envy gives you the chance to find out what you TRULY — and YOU-LY — want.

Which brings you to…

LIFE LESSON #20

When you're around people who have less, you tend to strive for less. But when you're with people who have what you crave, your spirit gets enlivened to find ways to hanker down and get what you crave.

When you think about this…you're reminded of an analogy…

AN ANALOGY IN A BOX
Whenever you play tennis with people who are better than you, you improve your game. Well, playing life with people who are better at playing life than you can also improve your life game.

When you think about this you are reminded of a little something ol' Bertolt Brecht once said:

" **Do not fear death.** Fear the inadequate life. "

Berty was right.
You must go out there and get what you want —
get it all, tiger!

Oh…while the getting is good, you must also be good and aware of how people might envy what good you got — and encourage their inner-tiger to go and get it too!

When you think about this you realize…

LIFE LESSON #21

What's so deadly about GLUTTONY? GLUTTONY IS ALL ABOUT A GENEROSITY OF SPIRIT… A POSITIVE OUTLOOK OF PLENTY AND BOUNTY… A PASSION FOR ALL LIFE HAS TO OFFER. Nothing deadly there, now is there?

GLUTTONY FEEDS YOUR SPIRIT with new experiences that have never been tried before…and some that have never been fried before.

Mmm…french fries…

French fries are a major spirit enlivener. In fact you're suspicious of people who don't like french fries…and puppies.

Yes, french fries and puppies are two of the world's most spirit enlivening treats.

You didn't always feel this way — at least about french fries. You used to view french fries as the enemy.

Yes, food to you was once simply a source for vitamins and minerals...not a source for pleasure and fun.

You used to view eating "bad foods" as showing "bad character."

You used to be one of the millions of the diet-obsessed people who contributed to the forty billion spent on dieting each year.

Not anymore.

Now…carbo is no longer a four-letter word… and you know how to spell "dessert" — with its full seven letters — "dessert" is not "desert." "DESSERT" is the one with two s's because you always want two…and, well, sometimes you now do have two, what the hell!

Brillat-Savarin, a French gastronome of the late eighteenth/early nineteenth century once said: "Tell me what you eat and I shall tell you what you are."

You now know…a person who shows a love for pleasurable foods is simultaneously revealing a love for a pleasurable life.

Which brings you to…

83

LIFE LESSON #22

GLUTTONY IS AN ATTITUDE, an attitude that's all about living life to its filled to the brim/brimming-over fullest. Gluttony is pro-non-norm, pro-non-status quo, pro-non-self-withholding, PRO-YOU GROWING….

And NOT JUST GROWING TO A BIGGER PANTS' SIZE —

BUT A BIGGER SPIRIT SIZE.

Gluttony can be about shoes as much as shoofly pie. Or one can be gluttonous for flowers, laughter, knowledge, creativity, travel — you want to taste it all.

Which brings you to...

LIFE LESSON #23

Similarly to lust...

GLUTTONY FOR A THING STOPS YOU IN TIME — STOPS YOU THINKING ABOUT THE PAST OR THE FUTURE — AND KEEPS YOU ALERT TO BEING FULLY PRESENT IN THE MMMMOOOOOOOOMENT.

You believe Mae West spoke for spirit as spirit incarnate when she said: "TOO MUCH OF A GOOD THING IS…WONDERFUL."

Yes, Mae had a point…a wonderful point. Gluttony is the spirit's way of showing a gluttony of spirit… a gluttony for fun…

So…how did gluttony get such a bad rap?

Ditto on: lust, greed, anger, pride, sloth, and envy?

Who's been spreading all these evil rumors?

Yes, it seems you're not the only SILLY YOU
out there who's bought into all this.

That's when you realize…

LIFE LESSON #24

The 7 deadly sins were set up to take the fall because THERE ARE REALLY 7 OTHER DEADLY SINS WHO FRAMED THEM ALL!

YES, CALL CNN…CALL *America's Most Wanted*…
CALL Court TV! The time has come to CAPTURE,
ACCUSE, AND BRING TO TRIAL THE TRUE 7 DEADLY
SINS RESPONSIBLE FOR CREATING THE LETHAL
SPIRIT SAPPING AND ZAPPING IN THIS WORLD!

AND THESE 7 BADDIES ARE…

1. EMOTIONAL MASOCHISM

2. GUILT

3. FEAR

4. REPRESSION OF SELF-EXPRESSION

5. NEED FOR SPEED

6. WORRY

7. APATHY

BOO! HISS! ON THESE BAD GUYS!

Those 7 SPIRIT KILLERS
have been bad-mouthing those 7 SPIRIT ENLIVENERS for years!

But now the time has come to come clean with the truth!

BAD-MOUTHING REMOVAL FORMULA

8.4 FL OZ / 250 ml

Which gets you thinking…

LIFE LESSON #25

You've got to make sure EMOTIONAL MASOCHISM doesn't stop you from seeking pleasure. But first you must seek the definition of EMOTIONAL MASOCHISM — and so you do...

THE DEFINITION OF EMOTIONAL MASOCHISM

Psychologists explain it as:

An instinctive universal self-sabotage syndrome we learn in childhood. As children, we grow up learning joy from our parents. If children learn joy in a joyless home, then as adults, too much joy can inspire anxiety…and the instinct to sabotage happiness in order to maintain one's learned, familiar masochistic equilibrium.

You describe it like this:

Hmmm….It's as if each of us grew up feeling comfortable with a certain quantity of happiness. Some of us are used to a 90 percent concentration…others only 75 percent…others only 17 percent. Whatever. The point is…when this concentration shifts — even if it's upward — and especially if it's upward — then a lot of us start to feel twitchy because this new zone feels sooo unfamiliar…and so we instinctively do what we must do to muck up our love or career lives so we can shift our happiness concentration back to our FAMILIAR childhood comfort — or rather DISCOMFORT — zone.

When you think about this you clearly see how

EMOTIONAL MASOCHISM has been masochistically keeping you from getting the higher level of ever-so-spirit-connecting exuberant love you want (ahem, LUST).

EMOTIONAL MASOCHISM has been masochistically keeping you from enjoying the higher level of ever-so-satisfying abundance you want (ahem, GREED).

EMOTIONAL MASOCHISM has been masochistically keeping you from enjoying the ever-so-yummy sensory-stimulation you want (ahem, GLUTTONY).

EMOTIONAL MASOCHISM has been masochistically keeping you from enjoying the ever-so-rejuvenating, ever-so-relaxing lifestyle you want (ahem, SLOTH).

EMOTIONAL MASOCHISM has been masochistically keeping you from recognizing your truest desires and being inspired to attain them (ahem, ENVY).

EMOTIONAL MASOCHISM has been masochistically keeping you from feeling okay about expressing (and not repressing) your ever-so-honest needs (ahem, ANGER).

EMOTIONAL MASOCHISM has been masochistically keeping you from reveling in whatever positive things you've managed to wrangle from the universe (ahem, PRIDE).

YES times 7...EMOTIONAL MASOCHISM has been stopping you sevenfold from enjoying your life, dammit!

Which leads you to...

LIFE LESSON #26

GUILT has also been PREVENTING YOU FROM ENJOYING YOUR LIFE, DAMMIT.

You once read in *The Pursuit of Pleasure*, by Lionel Tiger: "Pleasure and its availability loom as a resource, a lot like wealth. And like wealth, it's distributed to different groups, in different amounts."

When you read this you thought… hmmmm…women as a group have historically been allotted not such a lot of pleasure — in fact women are very much made to feel guilty for indulging in too much food, sex, money, power and fame.

And you've noticed how women who guiltlessly do ask for more and guiltlessly confront having gotten less are called bitches — tsk, tsk.

And it's funny how we have expressions like: "I feel so happy, I can't stand it." Or…"It's too much." Or…"I could die."

And expressions like: "Everything in moderation." And "Less is more." All suggesting: more = more guilt.

Then there's "No pain, no gain!"
Which also suggests there will be
"hell to pay"
for too much heaven.

All of this reminds you of something Ayn Rand once said, "The achievement of his own happiness is man's highest moral purpose."

Meaning?
It's your moral duty to eat that decadent candy on occasion.

GUILT SUCKS.

You shouldn't feel guilty for having it all. It's your moral perogative to have it all and be happy about it, baby.

It's time to give up those voices of self-conflict about pleasure.

After all, when you let yourself feel good you feel better about yourself and about life…and are thereby more open for love, intimacy, connection.

Which brings you to a mighty important life lesson...

LIFE LESSON #27

When you feel good…you're more likely to show goodwill.

Yes, you have more to give others when you allow yourself to guiltlessly give to yourself. Meaning? The pursuit of pleasure is not entirely a selfish act but a benefit to society…

WOOOOOOOOOOOOOOO-HOOOOOOOOOOOOOOOOOOO!

Which brings you to…

LIFE LESSON #28

FEAR has also been PREVENTING YOU FROM ENJOYING YOUR LIFE, DAMMIT.

Helen Keller said it loud and clear when she said, "Avoiding danger is no safer in the long run than outright exposure. The fearful are caught as often as the bold."

And so you realize you too must develop this Keller instinct toward fear.

And you know what you are instinctively afraid of — the same three things everyone on this planet is instinctively afraid of:

1. ■ anything new

2. ■ anything more

3. ■ anything different

Ironically the only way to grow and achieve greater happiness is to:

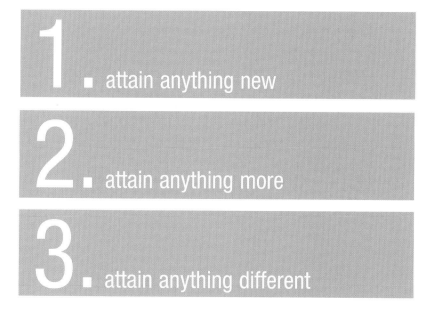

1. ■ attain anything new

2. ■ attain anything more

3. ■ attain anything different

You've read how the verb "to tempt" comes from the Latin word meaning "to stretch." Knowing this makes you smile…because you now realize that whenever you are lured into a new pleasure that tempts you in some way… you are simultaneously stretching yourself in some new way.

Yes, a new lover stretches you…not only in body…getting you to maybe stretch your limbs in ways you never thought possible. (Hmmmm, can a leg really go up there? You never thought a leg could do that before!)…But a new lover also gets you to stretch your heart and spirit in new ways. (Hmmm…can your heart really rise up that high? Geez, you never thought a heart could go so high before!)

All this reminds you of a lil' ditty from Anaïs Nin: "One's life shrinks or expands according to one's courage."

So, if you want an XL-life, with XL-spirit-expanding pleasure, you first and foremost need XL-courage.

Which gets you thinking…

LIFE LESSON #29

REPRESSION OF SELF-EXPRESSION has been PREVENTING YOU FROM ENJOYING YOUR LIFE, DAMMIT.

The good news is…

you have a say in what you get out
of your life…if you say what you want.

The bad news is…you MUST say what you want
out loud.*

Meaning? It's better to say difficult stuff now, rather
than try to fix difficult problems later. Yes, time
after time you've witnessed how the quality of
your communication equals the quality of
your life.

*Note: HOWEVER your darker thoughts MUST be said with good intentions!
Thanks! — This has been a message from the World Feelings Management Association.

What you don't ask for

...you don't get.*

*Duh.

And although you often might feel the people in your life

are from another planet,

unfortunately they are NOT of the Vulcan breed that can read your mind. If you want to be heard and understood, you must speaketh thyself up.*

*Note: And you must tryeth not to speaketh in annoyingeth Shakepeareanism for too longeth. Tis annoying, tis it not?

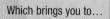
Which brings you to...

LIFE LESSON #30

THE NEED FOR SPEED has been PREVENTING YOU FROM ENJOYING YOUR LIFE, DAMMIT.

There was a time…a silly time…when you were a silly you… when you confused movement for forward motion…and you found that often you were simply spinning, spinning, spinning your wheels…and in this effort to keep moving you were sadly digging yourself in further…getting stuck in your same problem grooves instead of moving forward.

NOW you know: sometimes you've got to stop to go forward.

The longest distance between two points is reached by rushing.

You gotta relax, dammit.

You gotta pour yourself some bubbly while soaking in something bubbly…and soon you'll feel more bubbly… and have the energy and clarity to figure out how to get what you want.

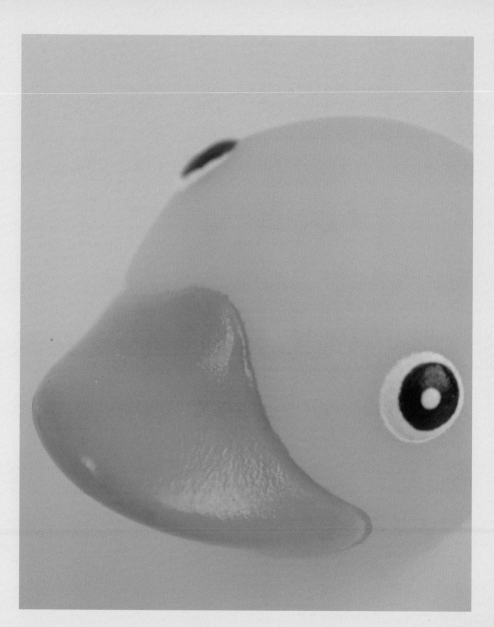

All of this reminds you of a story in Steven Covey's book *The Seven Habits of Highly Effective People*… which you'll summarize now in your own words.

SEEING THE SAW

There was this guy (GUY#1) who was sawing down a tree with a VERY long but dull saw…and so it was taking him a VERY long, dull time. His friend (GUY#2) tried to get him to stop sawing, and sharpen his saw. GUY#1 declined saying, "I can't take the time to sharpen the saw. I'm too busy sawing the tree."

Sadly, GUY#1 did not see what GUY#2 saw. You gotta slow down and sharpen the saw.

You see?

Basically, it's like this. There are always two reasons for doing anything:

1 ■ the right reason

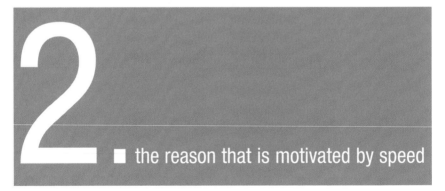

2 ■ the reason that is motivated by speed

And there are always two reasons for choosing the second reason:

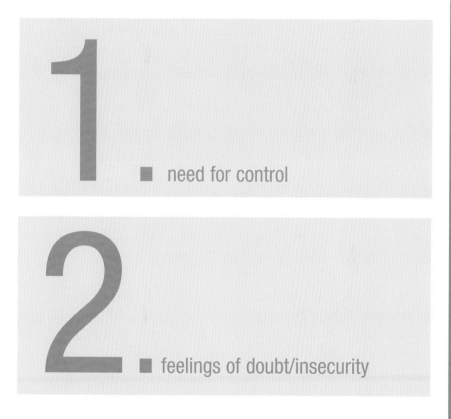

1.
■ need for control

2.
■ feelings of doubt/insecurity

In other words…you gotta learn to let go and trust yourself and the universe.

All of this reminds you of something Sir Isaac Newton once said: "If I have done the public any service it is due to patient thought."

You must be patient with your mind and stop bullying your neurons and allow them to lounge around a bit,

sip some chamomile tea...

put their little neuron feet up on little neuron-sized footstools, and release an aaaaah tiny neuron-sized sigh of relief...then you'll find that your neurons will find whatever thoughts you've been trying to wrestle from their grasp, and even give them up to you without all the tussle.

All of this reminds you of something Milan Kundera wrote about in his book *Slowness*.

A LITTLE BIT OF SLOWNESS QUICKLY

In his book, Kundera explains how we live in a speeded up culture — and this need for speed promotes forgetting. He explains how if a person wants to forget something, he will pick up speed walking down the street. If a person wants to remember something, he'll slow down his steps. And speeding up in general makes a person not only forget specific things, but basic values and ideals for how to live an enjoyable, rewarding, passion-filled life.

So…when you see people walking really quickly down the street, they are literally running from themselves.

Which brings you to…

LIFE LESSON #31

WORRY has been PREVENTING YOU FROM ENJOYING YOUR LIFE, DAMMIT.

Unfortunately we live in a world of uncertainty —
and unfortunately when you stop to think about
it — if you have time to stop — if you're not too
stressed to stop — and if you are too stressed,
then you should definitely stop — so STOP!! —
anyway, you realize that a synonym of sorts for

"uncertainty" is "stress."

And even more unfortunately, as a human
you often find yourself uncertain and thereby
certainly stressed when you should be living
right here comfortably present in your present.

Which reminds you of something that righteous babe Ann Magnuson once said, "When you have one foot on your past, and one foot on your future, you wind up peeing all over your present."

In other words:
BE HERE NOW...
don't pee here now.

But speaking of your past…there was a time waaaay back…back when you were a silly you, when you confused worry for preparation.

But now you know better.

Now you know:

WORRY IS A HAZARDOUS TIME-WASTE MATERIAL.

Worry gets annoying, blurring, distracting toxic thought dust all over your finest hours.

Worry not only distracts…it attracts. It winds up veering you right smack into the very thing you worried about smacking into.

Which reminds you of a good analogy...

A GOOD ANALOGY IN A BOX
Race car drivers know that you should never look at that wall you fear squooshing your nice, shiny race car into — because wherever you're looking IS where your race car aims itself. So, you should keep your eye only on the places you want to be and go!

Which brings you to…

LIFE LESSON #32

APATHY has also been
PREVENTING YOU FROM
ENJOYING YOUR LIFE, DAMMIT.

When you think about this you think about a famous Ralph Waldo Emerson quote, "Nothing great was ever achieved without enthusiasm...and lots of double frapuccinos."

Er...um...or he said something like that.

Hmmm, actually, Emerson was alive BEFORE Starbucks.*

So...you suppose Emerson never got to benefit from all that double frapuccino stuff.

Meaning?

Poor Emerson had to depend solely on enthusiasm as his one and only guiding gusto.

And you know you too MUST very much depend on enthusiasm to get the life you want.

*Note: Yes, there WAS a time BEFORE Starbucks.

Yes, you must not sit around all complacent and wait for an exceptional life to just find you. Taking no action IS an action. If you are doing nothing to move your life forward, you are still doing something, by making the decision to remain in the same place.

So indirectly, inaction is an action. You must act or be acted upon.

You must pick up that bat, and start a-swinging…

and be ready to run.

And if you're gonna swing…you must swing hard. And if you're gonna run…then you must run hard. And if you're gonna wanna steal second…then you can't lull around on first base forever. You must move your toosh, dammit.

Fortunately, you know where this frozen-toosh/apathy/inaction stuff comes from:

1. fear of failure

2. fear of success

Only you're not sure which of those two you're more afraid of.

But you do know that either way, with either fear, there's a two-tiered solution to achieving what you want:

1. You must believe in your abilities.

2. You must believe in your worthiness.

Which brings you to…

LIFE LESSON #33

IT'S NOT ENOUGH TO MILDLY WANT WHAT YOU WANT. YOU MUST WILDLY WANT WHAT YOU WANT.

No one ever got their greatest wishes
by remaining wishy-washy. There are
no wishy-washy CEOs, no wishy-washy
astronauts, no wishy-washy rock stars.

The universe rewards the decisive.
The universe rewards the enthusiastic.
The greater your decisiveness, the
greater your enthusiasm, the greater
your "LUCK" in getting what you want.

And you know what it is you want: all that good spirit
enlivening stuff all those 7 spirit enliveners bring you!

And that's when you realize…

LIFE LESSON #34

Repent oh sinner...

for the sin of NOT sinning in LUST, GREED, ANGER, PRIDE, SLOTH, ENVY, GLUTTONY. Release your EMOTIONAL MASOCHISM, GUILT, FEAR, REPRESSION OF SELF-EXPRESSION, NEED FOR SPEED, WORRY, and APATHY...

and enliven your life!

Consider the following EXAMPLES…starting with…

LIFE LESSON #35

You need to enliven your life with more LUST! YOU MUST MERRILY TAKE YOUR SPIRIT TO THE LUST AND FOUND... FIND AS MUCH LUST AS YOU CAN TO FILL YOUR LIFE, BEDROOM, KITCHEN, HALLWAY, SHOWER...

YES...you must make sure you have
more hot showers you share with a loved one...
than cold showers you retreat to alone.

And at bedtime, if you're having trouble sleeping, it's always nice to hear a good NC-17 bedtime story — told to you by your loved one…to help you sleep…or better yet…to have a reason to stay awake (wink,wink).

And when you (wink,wink) DO stay awake, you must stay FULLY awake and not sleepwalk through your motions and emotions…so you can truly connect. You must consciously decide to be FULLY aware of ALL your sensual senses sensing what they sense — FULLY seeing, smelling, tasting, hearing, feeling — and also eeling for — your paramour.

You must consciously decide to be 100 percent mindfully and bodyfully present in lust.

For another example…

LIFE LESSON #36

You need to enliven your life with more GREED! YOU MUST LET GO OF ANY NEGATIVE ASSOCIATIONS YOU HAVE TOWARD MONEY, AND WATCH IT ZOOM TOWARD YOU.

And as the money zooms in, remember: you must not only have a balanced checkbook, but a balanced life of spending and investing. BOTH your money and your lifestyle enjoyment should be increasing simultaneously. Invest in both mutual funds (see your broker) and mutual fun (see your travel agent and book a trip to Hawaii with your paramour!).

Also remember, we live in a world of abundance.
There's plenty to go around. So let it go…

and it will go around…and around…back to you. Yes, money has

major karmic boomerang benefits.

So be sure to give a little something to your favorite
charity each year.

Which brings you to…

LIFE LESSON #37

You need to enliven your life with more ANGER! Aggression is better than repression.

When anger is properly channeled it's a force to be reckoned with to accomplish your goals.

So write that letter to your local congressman or congresswoman about what you want to see change within your community — then mail it ASAP!

And write that speech to your boss about how you've had it with the chump change you've been getting paid — then memorize your speech — and raise the issue of your raise — ASAP!

And if you're a woman,
memorize this while you're at it:

BEHIND MANY A SUCCESSFUL WOMAN IS SOMEONE WHO PISSED HER OFF.

Meaning?

You must wisely channel your anger to forge forward to get what you want — reminding yourself that success will be the best revenge on all those not rooting for you.

With this in mind, keep in mind: it helps to write a list of those non-rooters — people who have angered you — and keep this non-rooter list nearby knowing

HATE PREVENTS LATE.

This non-rooter list can rile you to action, reminding you how your non-rooters would want you to procrastinate — and not get what you want — and so you must stop procrastinating and get what you want, so as to give a big nyah-nyah to your non-rooters!

Which brings you to…

LIFE LESSON #38

You need to enliven your life with more PRIDE!

You must consciously decide now to banish that whiny self-critical voice within and show yourself some self-respect by listening to your self-loving self instead.

You must consciously remember to remind yourself about all the good you've brought into your life — like this BOOK!

Yes, clever lil' you brought this book to lucky lil' you — a peppy, cheery, self-love-promoting book that reminds you to focus on and enjoy all the good you have...and NOT stay blurry-eyed on what you don't have. BECAUSE WHAT YOU SEE IS WHAT YOU GET! SO IF YOU SEE GOOD IN YOUR LIFE, YOU GET MORE GOOD IN YOUR LIFE!

Damn I'm good,
Damn I'm good,
Damn I'm good,
Damn I'm good,

You must consciously decide NOW to maintain an **attitude of gratitude** morning, noon, and night.

Damn I'm good,
Damn I'm good,
Damn I'm good,

Damn I'm good,
Damn I'm good,
Damn I'm good,
Damn I'm good,

You must consciously decide NOW
to compliment yourself internally
after every positive step forward.

Damn I'm good,

You must consciously decide NOW to
memorize this mantra: "Damn I'm good,
Damn I'm good, Damn I'm good, Damn
I'm good." And use this mantra frequently
in your future.

Damn I'm good,

And when it comes to your past, a good way to remind yourself of how far you've come, is to surround yourself with all you've accomplished.

Soooo…put out all those photos that capture your moments of past glory… or keep in eyesight those awards you've received.

Heck, start putting gold stars in your calendar on days you've accomplished something BIG. Then decide that in upcoming years you'll celebrate these days as Personal Self Holidays along with birthdays and anniversaries.

Which brings you to…

LIFE LESSON #39

You need to enliven your life with more SLOTH! BED DOES NOT EQUAL BAD. BED EQUALS TIME TO RELAX AND THINK AND REJUVENATE. AND JUMPING INTO BED ISN'T JUST ABOUT PASSION…BUT SELF-COMPASSION… ESPECIALLY WHEN YOU JUMP INTO BED ALONE WITH A BIG, HARD, LONG BOOK… AND READ, READ, READ.

So decide now to go out and buy yourself some new throw pillows — fancy ones, with ruffles, made of velvet and filled with fluffy feathers — then nestle your weary neck upon some of them, and your weary feet upon the rest…and give your brain a rest.

Let the dishes soak in the sink.

Sleep an extra half hour in the morning.

Schedule cozy and comfy times with someone you love.

Remember:
You're called a human being — not a
human doing. You don't always have to be

doing, doing, doing, doing.

In fact, doing too much is often a
way of doing too little of what you
really have to do.

Which brings you to…

LIFE LESSON #40

You need to enliven your life with more ENVY! Perk up and pay attention to what makes you envious — then use this feeling to propel you to get this thing — knowing if someone else got it, then (yeeha!) that means it's possible to get!

Don't settle for less than your envy invites you to drool over.

You must follow your drool!

Um…er…which is a grosser way of saying what Joseph Campbell once said: "Follow your bliss."

And if you're following your bliss into an article in some magazine — and you find yourself reading about someone who somehow snagged your drool-worthy bliss for their own little life — well, don't read it and weep — read it and reap.

Clip this article and keep it nearby to keep you self-honest about what you want for yourself — and empowered and inspired and motivated to get this drool-worthy bliss for your life too.

Which brings you to…

LIFE LESSON #41

You need to enliven your life with more GLUTTONY!

You must decide right now to be hyperaware of every gustatory nuanced bite that greets your taste bud laden tongue.

You know… when you eat more slowly you need to eat less often.

You know…you must never eat when upset or distracted…because you won't get the full gluttonous rewards from your food.

And you've got to stop feeling that everything that tastes good is bad.

Mangoes, cherries, portobello mushrooms, oysters on the half shell — these are all treats with the trick of being good for you.

And when it comes to gluttony, it's not just what you eat —

it's where you eat it.

Indulge thyself while in bed.

Eat that Chinese food directly from the container while watching *Sex and the City*.

Speaking of...

And on occasion, hell, don't share…your dessert.
You CAN be too thin…so go eat something too rich.

Yes, it's okay to pig out on occasion.

And not just when it comes to eating. You should pig out on traveling, reading, movie-watching, sailing, antiquing — whatever your indulgence, INDULGE!

Remember: The only thing in moderation should be my mother.
(Note: Sorry, Mom. But there you have it.)

Which brings you to...

LIFE LESSON #42

Wow, so much to enliven your life with, so little time to enliven it up in.

It's up to you to use your time well.

It's up to you to decide right now you will be a pleasure-directed person...not a pain-directed person.

PLEASURE-DIRECTED PEOPLE

lead their lives by being motivated to move toward pleasure…rather than running from pain.

PLEASURE-DIRECTED PEOPLE

are inspired by what interests them, enthuses them, inspires them.

PLEASURE-DIRECTED PEOPLE

are less likely to be controlling, vindictive, snooty, competitive…because they are happier, more balanced, more centered… and thereby they attract more positive circumstances — and more positive, loving people too.

And so you think about this — and realize (CLUNK!)

LIFE LESSON #43

It's waaaaay better to lead a PLEASURE-DIRECTED life — for you and everyone else around you. And it's waaaaay better for you — and everyone else around you — to allow yourself to enjoy all this pleasure that you direct your way!

EVERYONE BENEFITS
FROM YOUR HAPPINESS.

ALTHOUGH — DUH — YOU
ESPECIALLY BENEFIT FROM
YOUR HAPPINESS…IF YOU
LET YOURSELF.

AND SO YOU MUST — DUH — LET YOURSELF.

You must know and appreciate that your life doesn't have to be ENTERPAINING in order for it be interesting, pleasurable, and enjoyable.

You can have your life be interesting, pleasurable, and enjoyable and your life can still be very much interesting, pleasurable, and enjoyable.

IT'S ALL UP TO...

YOU.

Which brings you to…

LIFE LESSON #44

You — and you alone — are in charge of creating that movie-for-one called your life. You — and you alone — are not only your own life writer, but life casting agent, director, producer, caterer, everything-er. IF YOU DON'T LIKE YOUR LIFE MOVIE…if you feel it's too much ENTERPAINMENT and not enough ENTERTAINMENT…then it's up to YOU — and YOU alone — to close down the movie set and re-cast and re-shoot…and not waste another day shooting scenes that would be better off on the editing room floor.

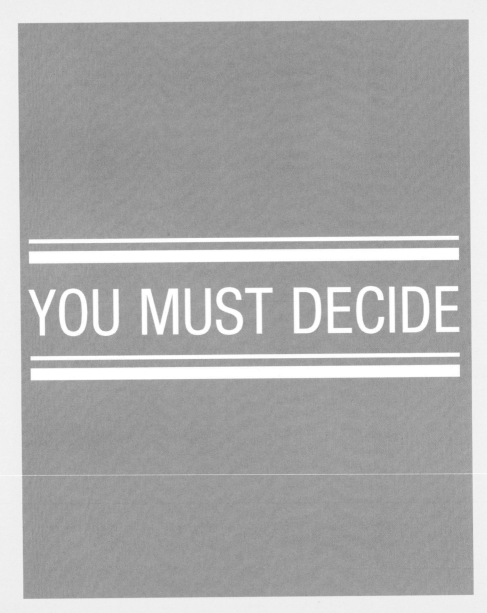

ENOUGH WITH THE ENTERPAINMENT ALREADY!

IT'S VERY OKAY TO GIVE

YOURSELF A HAPPY ENDING.

And may you live

happily ever after...

MIT!

the 7 lively sins